Mean Machines

SUPER CARS

Q2ABillSmith

Created by Q2ABillSmith
www.qbslearning.com
Text, design & illustrations Copyright © Q2AMedia 2012

Scholastic and Tangerine Press and associated logos are trademarks and/or registered trademarks of Scholastic Inc.

an imprint of
■ SCHOLASTIC
www.scholastic.com

Published by Tangerine Press, an imprint of Scholastic Inc., 557 Broadway; New York, NY 10012

Scholastic Canada Ltd.; Markham, Ontario
Scholastic Australia Pty. Ltd.; Gosford NSW
Scholastic New Zealand Ltd.; Greenmount, Auckland

Author Geoff Barker
Editor Honor Head
Client Service Manager Ravneet Kaur
Project Manager Summit Kumar
Creative Director Joita Das
Designer Souvik Mukherjee and Roshan
Picture Researcher Ranjana Batra and Farheen Aadil

10 9 8 7 6 5 4 3 2 1

ISBN: 978-0-545-43104-0

Printed in Shenzhen, China.

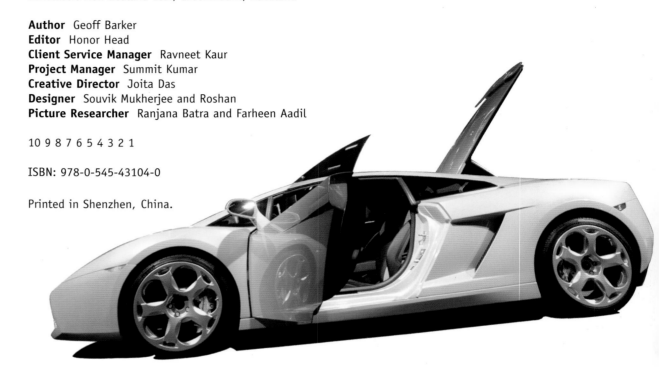

Picture Credits

t= top, b= bottom, c= centre, r= right, l= left

Cover Page: Ron Kimball/KimballStock
Back Cover: Rex Features
Title Page: A163/Gamma-Rapho/Getty Images
Content Page: Pagani Automobili S.p.a

4: Dag Ohrlund/Rex Features; 5tl: Solent News/Rex Features; 5b: Erik Pendzich/Rex/Features; 6: Laurent Cipriani/AP Photo; 7tl: Pagani Automobili S.p.a; 7b: David McNew/Getty Images; 8: Ga la/Imaginechina/AP Images; 9: Jochen Eckel/Bloomberg/Getty Images; P10: Pagani Automobili S.p.a; P11t: Pagani Automobili S.p.a; P11b: Pagani Automobili S.p.a; 12-13: Indranil Mukherjee/AFP/Getty Images; 13t: Indranil Mukherjee/AFP/Getty Images; 13b: KeystoneUSA-ZUMA/Rex Features; 14tr: Junko Kimura/Getty Images; 14bl: Torsten Silz/AFP/Getty Images; 15: Car Culture/Getty Images; 16: ImageBroker/Rex Features; 17tl: Adrian Moser/Bloomberg/Getty Images; 17b: ImageBroker/Rex Features; 18: RGE Robert Gülpen Engineering/Rex Features; 19tr: KeystoneUsa-Zuma/Rex Features; 19bl: Joffet Emmanuel/SIPA/Rex Features; 20-21: Stan Honda/AFP/Getty Images; 21tr: Stan Honda/AFP/Getty Images; 21br: J. Emilio Flores/Getty Images; 22: Stan Honda/AFP/Getty Images; 23: Car Culture/Getty Images; 24: KPA/Zuma/Rex Feature; 25tr: Mike Fanous/Gamma-Rapho/Getty Images; 25b: KPA/Zuma/Rex Features; 26: China Photos/Getty Images; 27tl: Car Culture/Getty Images; 27b: Thomas Coex/AFP/Getty Images; 28: Kristie Bull/Graylock.com/AP Photo; 29tl: Neale Haynes/Rex Features; 29b: Jonathan Fickies/Getty Images; 30: Solent News/Rex Features; 31t: Rex Features; 31b: Jung Yeon-Je/AFP/Getty Images; 32tl: Solent News/Rex Features; 32b: Action Press/Rex Features; 33: Solent News/Rex Features; 34: Jim Watson/AFP/Getty Images; 35tr: Rex Features; 35: Robert Timoney/Rex Features; 36: Joerg Koch/AFP/Getty Images; 37: Pascal Le Segretain/Getty Images; 38: Rinspeed/Rex Features; 39: Unimedia South America/Rex Features; 40t: Yousef Allan/AP Photo; 40b: Charles M. Ommanney/Rex Features; 41: Eric Risberg/AP Photo; 42: Virginia Sherwood/NBC/NBCU Photo Bank/Getty Images; 43tr: MB Pictures/Rex Features; 43br: Beverly News/Rex Features; 45tr: Pagani Automobili S.p.a

Contents

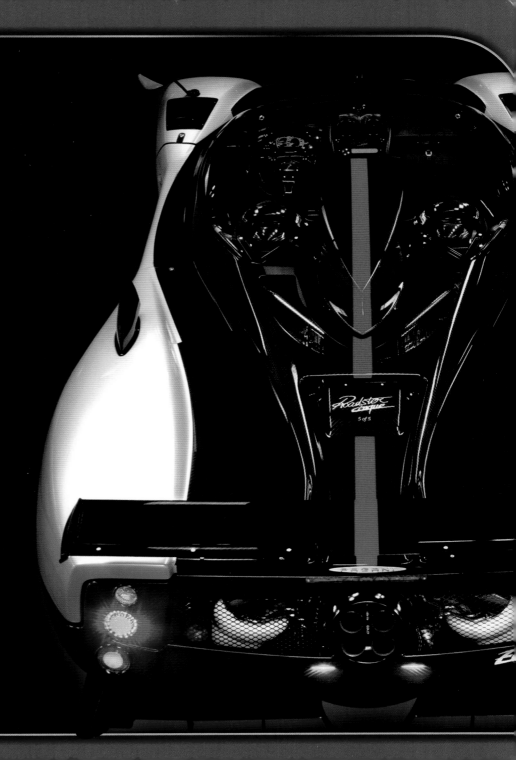

What Is a Supercar?

In a class of their own, **supercars** are things of beauty. They are sleek, shiny, fast, and powerful. These awesome vehicles are owned by the superstars of sports and movies. If you want to see some super cool and really awesome cars, read on!

▼ *The Modena Spyder supercar looks just like a classic 1961 Ferrari 250 GT California Spyder.*

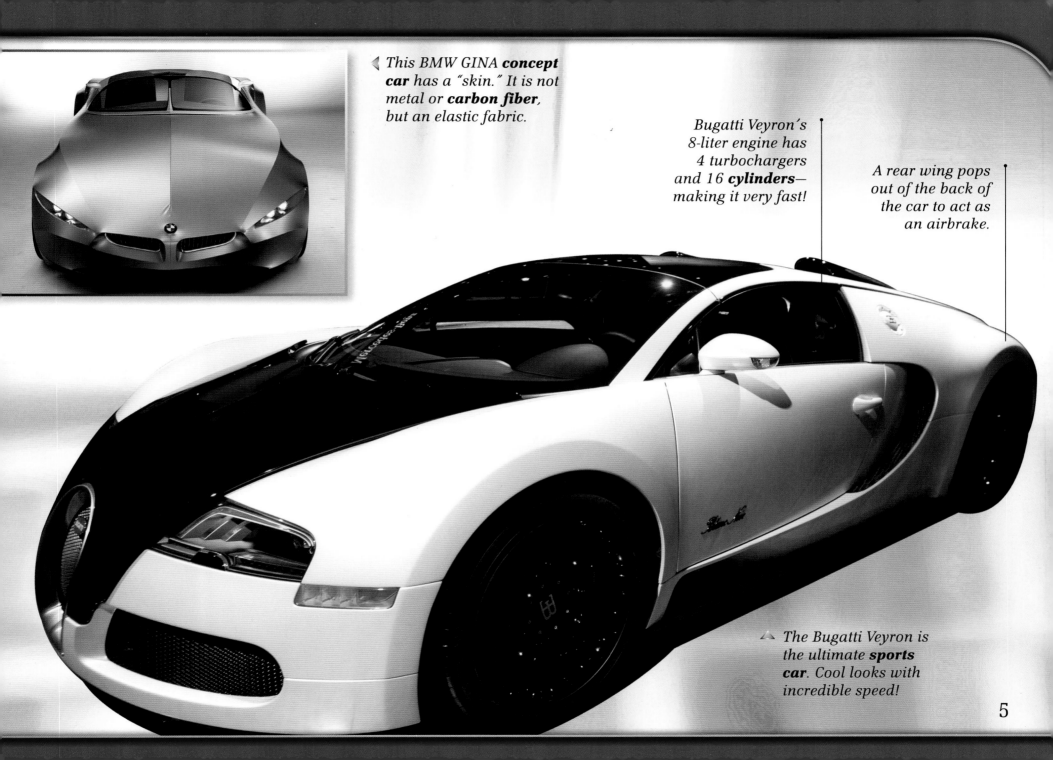

This BMW GINA **concept car** has a "skin." It is not metal or **carbon fiber**, but an elastic fabric.

Bugatti Veyron's 8-liter engine has 4 turbochargers and 16 **cylinders**—making it very fast!

A rear wing pops out of the back of the car to act as an airbrake.

The Bugatti Veyron is the ultimate **sports car**. Cool looks with incredible speed!

Most Expensive Supercars

Imagine hurtling along straight roads at crazy speeds. All of these supercars can reach speeds over 200 **mph** (322 **kph**). Power, speed, and style do not come cheap. Which supercar do you think is the most expensive? Let's find out.

▽ *This amazing supercar is a Bugatti Veyron Super Sport.*

The mega engine leaves no room for passengers in the back.

*Supercars need sports car wheels fitted with **low-profile tires**.*

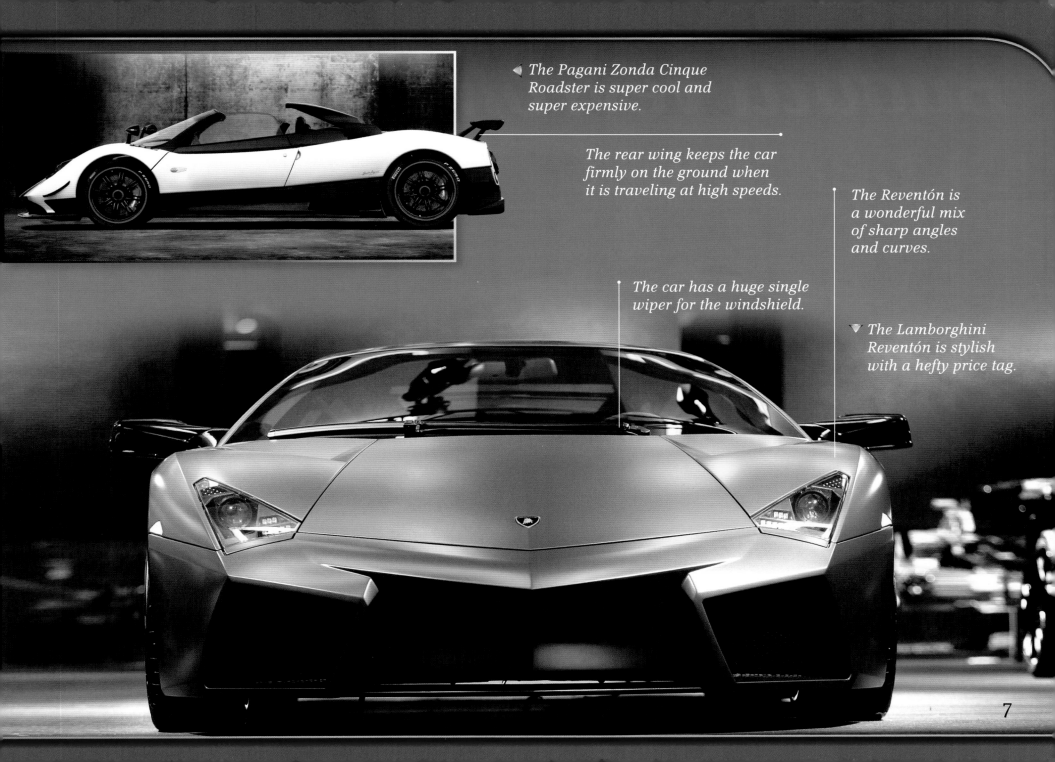

◀ The Pagani Zonda Cinque Roadster is super cool and super expensive.

The rear wing keeps the car firmly on the ground when it is traveling at high speeds.

The Reventón is a wonderful mix of sharp angles and curves.

The car has a huge single wiper for the windshield.

▼ The Lamborghini Reventón is stylish with a hefty price tag.

Bugatti Veyron Super Sport

The Veyron 16.4 car has 16 cylinders that give this car its incredible power.

What is so special about the **limited edition** Bugatti Veyron Super Sport? It's beautiful, powerful, fast, and the most expensive **production car** money can buy. It is named for the French racing driver Pierre Veyron, "winner of the 1939 Le Mans." Very few of these cars are made each year. So, they are difficult to find and extremely expensive.

"Bugatti" is named for Ettore Bugatti, founder of the company.

COOL FACTS

- Car: Veyron Super Sport
- Top speed: 268 mph (431 kph)
- 0–60 mph (96.6 kph): 2.5 seconds
- Power: 1,200 **bhp**
- Engine: 8-liter **W16**
- **Transmission**: 7-speed
- **Cost**: $2.4 million

You can recognize the Super Sport by its signature black and orange paint job.

The Super Sport's carbon-fiber skin was first used in 2010.

▼ *The Bugatti Veyron Super Sport first appeared in 2010.*

Pagani Zonda Cinque Roadster

Horacio Pagani wanted to create the most beautiful car in the world. He became successful making carbon-fiber parts for supercars, and then he got to live out his dream. In 1993, at the age of 37, Pagani began a long project—to build his very own supercar, the Pagani Zonda. His special supercar took more than six years to make. Then, Pagani went on to build the Zonda Cinque Roadster, which will cost you almost $2 million.

*This roadster is a **convertible** car: The roof can be taken off.*

▼ *Only five Pagani Zonda Cinque Roadsters were ever built.*

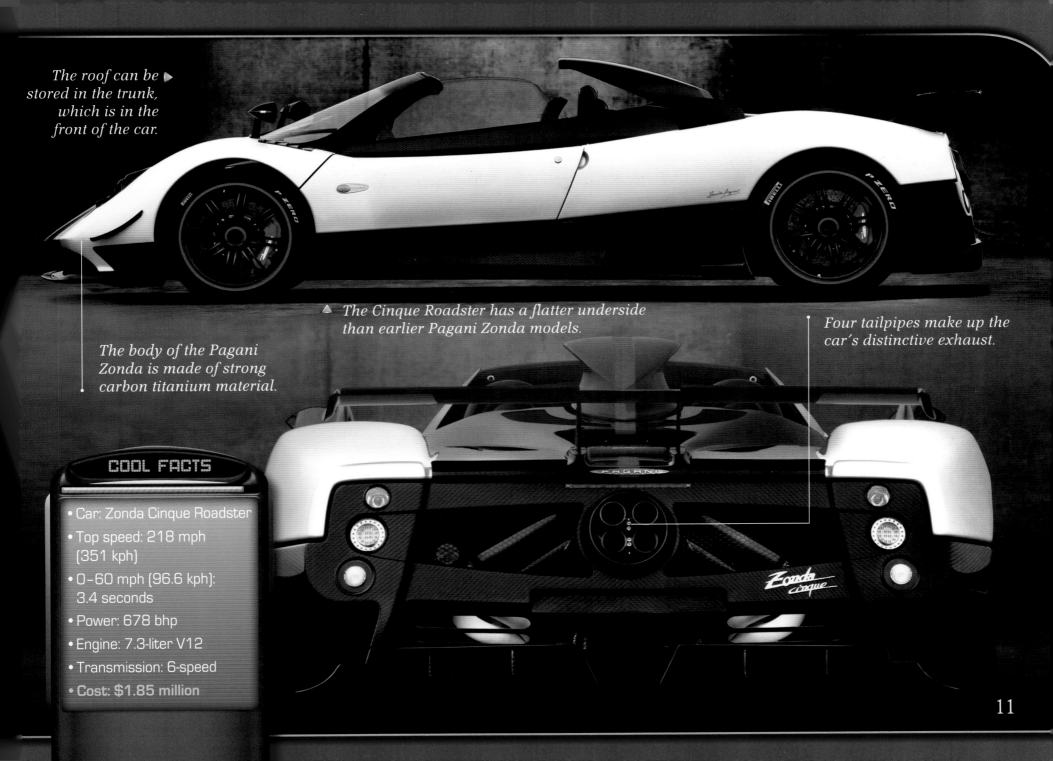

The roof can be stored in the trunk, which is in the front of the car.

The body of the Pagani Zonda is made of strong carbon titanium material.

The Cinque Roadster has a flatter underside than earlier Pagani Zonda models.

Four tailpipes make up the car's distinctive exhaust.

COOL FACTS

- Car: Zonda Cinque Roadster
- Top speed: 218 mph (351 kph)
- 0–60 mph (96.6 kph): 3.4 seconds
- Power: 678 bhp
- Engine: 7.3-liter V12
- Transmission: 6-speed
- Cost: $1.85 million

Aston Martin One-77

Stylish supercar **manufacturer** Aston Martin unveiled the gorgeous One-77 in 2009. The car's unusual name means that this is a limited-edition car with only 77 cars made— and each car is built to be unique. The usual big **V8** Aston Martin engine has been replaced by an enormous **V12** engine. It can actually fit a mega 7.3 liters of air into all of its 12 cylinders.

COOL FACTS

- Car: One-77
- Top speed: 220 mph (354 kph)
- 0–60 mph (96.6 kph): 3.5 seconds
- Power: 750 bhp
- Engine: 7.3-liter V12
- Transmission: 6-speed manual gears
- Cost: $1.85 million

The design of the One-77 ▷ blends beauty with speed and performance.

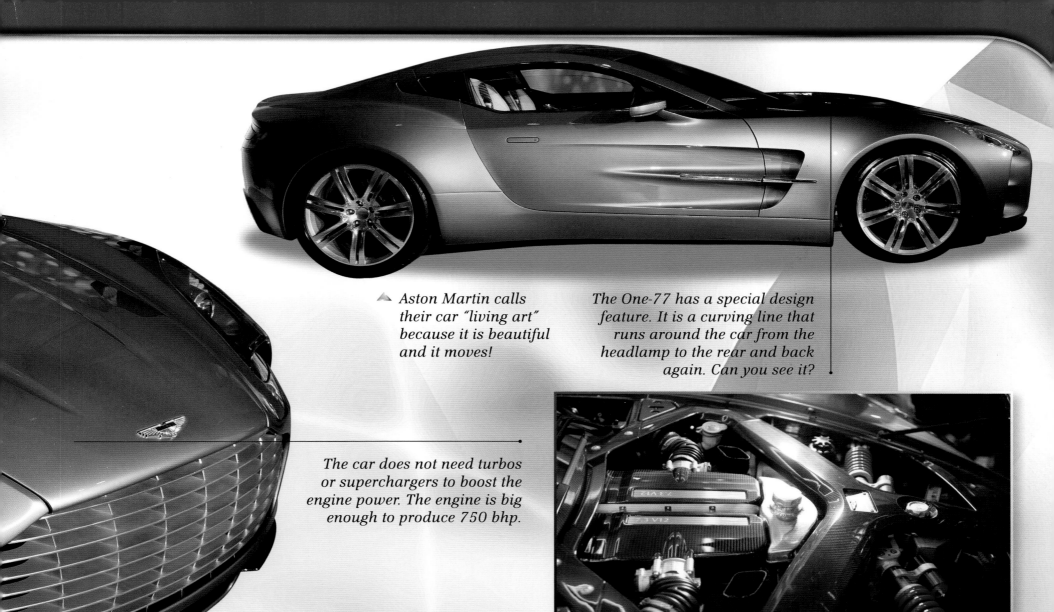

▲ Aston Martin calls
their car "living art"
because it is beautiful
and it moves!

The One-77 has a special design
feature. It is a curving line that
runs around the car from the
headlamp to the rear and back
again. Can you see it?

The car does not need turbos
or superchargers to boost the
engine power. The engine is big
enough to produce 750 bhp.

All that power in the engine ▷
makes a tremendous roar!

13

Lamborghini Reventón

In 1963, Lamborghini started building supercool Italian sports cars. Named for a bull that killed a famous matador, the stylish Reventón is similar to the successful Murciélago but isn't as curvy. Lamborghini's designers have built a striking new car with a look based on the world's fastest airplanes, making the Reventón a mean-looking speed machine. It is two parts car and one part **stealth fighter jet!**

Doors open upwards—a Lamborghini feature.

All Reventóns come in gray-green. Although the surface is not shiny, tiny metallic particles can reflect the sunlight.

The large air intake on the driver's side helps increase the flow of oil to the car's radiator.

This is the Lamborghini Murciélago LP640. The Reventón is based on this cool car.

14

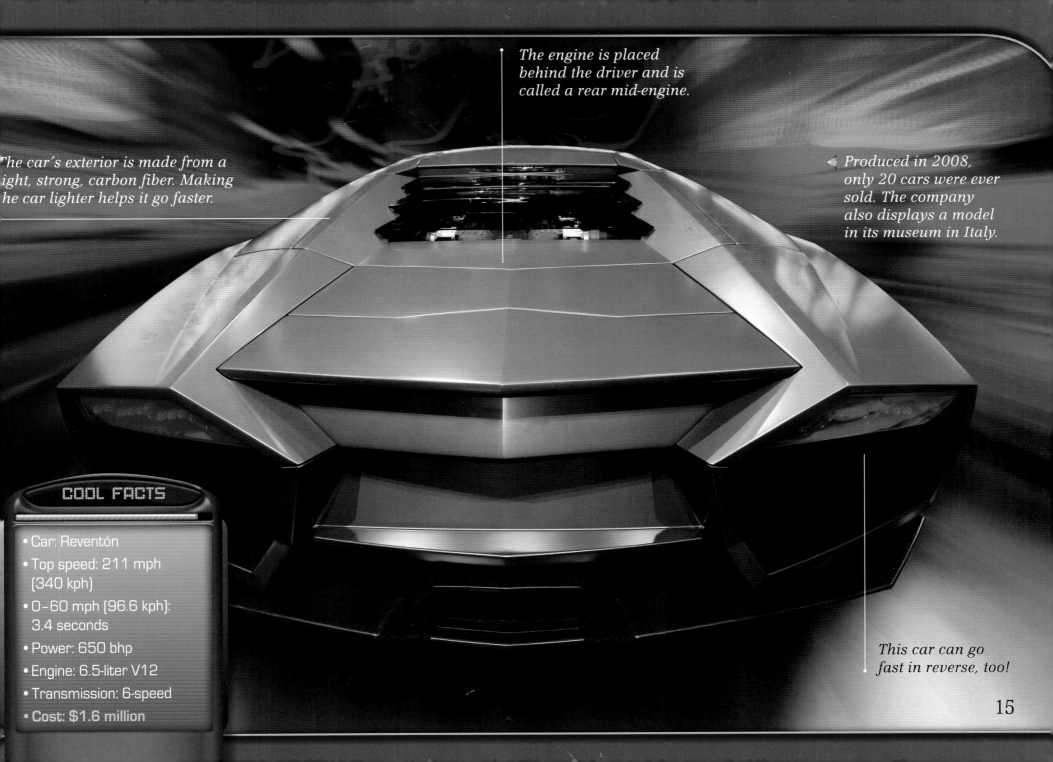

The engine is placed behind the driver and is called a rear mid-engine.

The car's exterior is made from a light, strong, carbon fiber. Making the car lighter helps it go faster.

Produced in 2008, only 20 cars were ever sold. The company also displays a model in its museum in Italy.

COOL FACTS

- Car: Reventón
- Top speed: 211 mph (340 kph)
- 0–60 mph (96.6 kph): 3.4 seconds
- Power: 650 bhp
- Engine: 6.5-liter V12
- Transmission: 6-speed
- Cost: $1.6 million

This car can go fast in reverse, too!

Koenigsegg Agera R

Imagine you want to buy one of the most expensive supercars in the world. Pack your bags and take a trip to Sweden, the home of **hypercar** newcomer Koenigsegg. Their supercar, the CCX, is stunning, but the new Koenigsegg Agera R tops even that. This car recently made a Guinness World Record by traveling from 0 to 186 mph (299 kph) and back to 0 in 21.19 seconds. The company claims that the car can reach a mind-blowing 273 mph (439 kph), but this has not yet been verified.

▼ *The Koenigsegg Agera R's body is made of a tough carbon-Kevlar material.*

COOL FACTS

- Car: Agera R
- Top speed: 273 mph (439 kph) [unverified]
- 0–60 mph (96.6 kph): 2.9 seconds
- Power: 1,115 bhp
- Engine: 5.0-liter twin-turbo V8
- Transmission: 7-speed
- Cost: $1.6 million

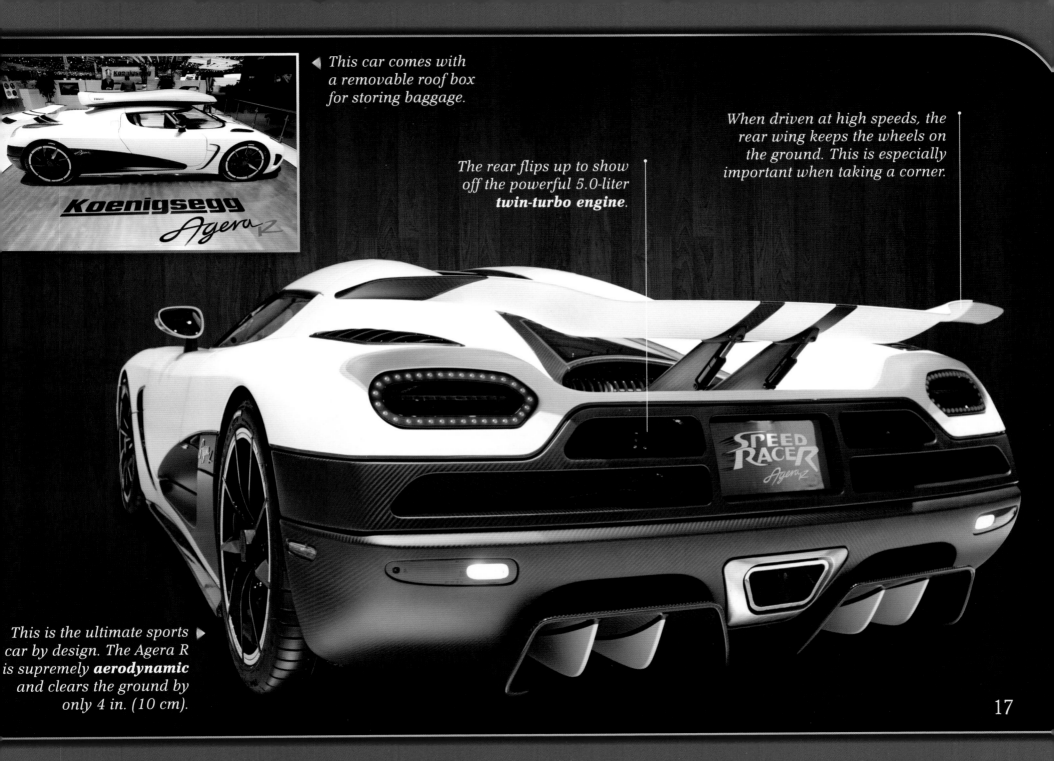

This car comes with a removable roof box for storing baggage.

When driven at high speeds, the rear wing keeps the wheels on the ground. This is especially important when taking a corner.

The rear flips up to show off the powerful 5.0-liter **twin-turbo engine**.

Koenigsegg Agera R

This is the ultimate sports car by design. The Agera R is supremely **aerodynamic** and clears the ground by only 4 in. (10 cm).

SPEED RACER Agera R

Wish List Cars

Hatchbacks and **sedans** are all right for a ride to school, but if you were a millionaire, wouldn't you want to be driven in a supercar? Which car would top your list? Supercars, like the Lamborghini or Ferrari? Or would you rather go with the classy Rolls-Royce or Maybach?

Front-hinged scissor doors are perfect for special occasions so celebrities can make a dramatic entrance.

▽ *The Lamborghini Aventador LP700-4 has a top speed of 217 mph (349 kph). It goes 0–60 mph (96.6 kph) in under 3 seconds.*

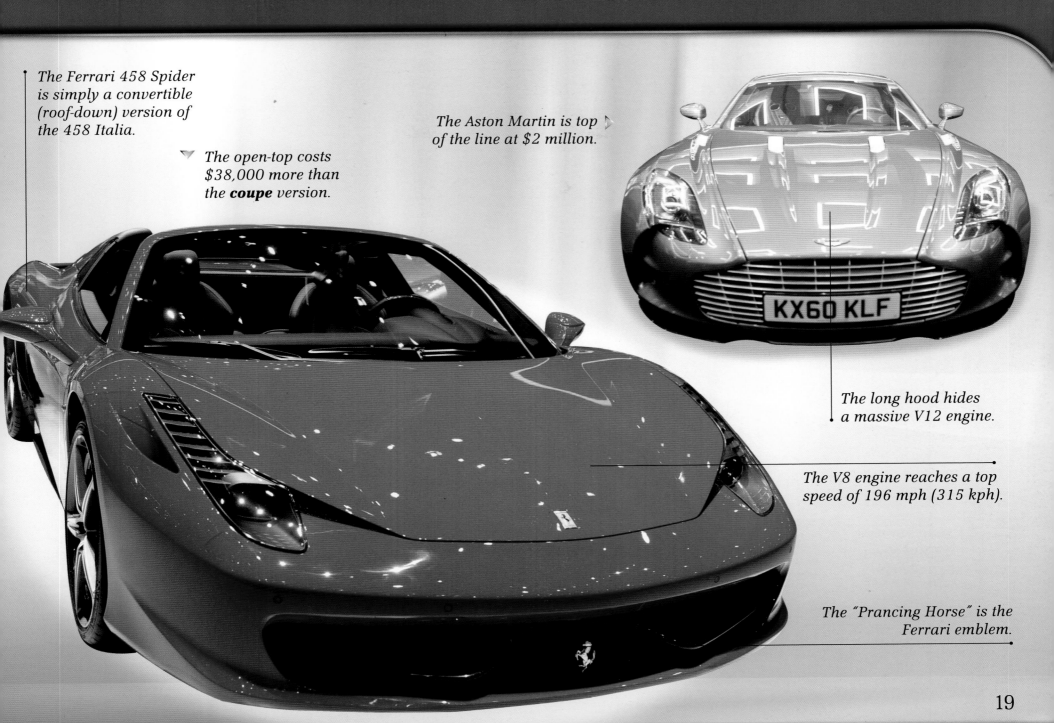

The Ferrari 458 Spider is simply a convertible (roof-down) version of the 458 Italia.

The open-top costs $38,000 more than the **coupe** version.

The Aston Martin is top of the line at $2 million.

The long hood hides a massive V12 engine.

The V8 engine reaches a top speed of 196 mph (315 kph).

The "Prancing Horse" is the Ferrari emblem.

19

Lamborghini Gallardo Spyder

Lamborghini recently sold its 12,000th Gallardo. However, the Lamborghini Gallardo Spyder convertible coupe is super cool and different, too. When it was launched in 2005, it was voted the world's most beautiful car by an international jury of car experts in Milan, Italy.

COOL FACTS

- Car: Gallardo Spyder
- Top speed: 195 mph (314 kph)
- 0–60 mph (100 kph): 3.4 seconds
- Power: 520 bhp
- Engine: 5.2-liter V10
- Transmission: 6-speed
- Cost: $250,000

◀ *The Gallardo Spyder has everything, including a soft top for cool drives on sunny days.*

Powerful lights stare out from the edges of the angled front end.

*The 5.2-liter engine is behind the driver. This is the **hard-top** version of the car.*

Maybach 62 S

If you want quality, the Maybach 62 S is an expensive sedan that always looks good. Tell your **chauffeur** where you want to go and stretch out your legs in the super-roomy extended body. The Maybach is a powerful high-tech machine. Originally, Maybach was its own company. Now, the cars are manufactured by Mercedes-Benz.

Under the massive hood lies a twin turbo-charged V12 engine. This luxury car is capable of going from 0 to 60 mph (96.6 kph) in just over 5 seconds.

COOL FACTS

- Car: Maybach 62 S
- Top speed: 155 mph (249 kph)
- 0–60 mph (96.6 kph): 5.2 seconds
- Power: 620 bhp
- Engine: 6-liter V12
- Transmission: 5-speed automatic
- Cost: $450,000

Check out the luxury! Only the very best leather is luxurious enough for these individual back seats that you can adjust at the flick of a switch.

23

Rolls-Royce Phantom Drophead Coupe

The Drophead Coupe has a special hand-built aluminum frame. Aluminum is a light but tough metal.

The drop top is down. "Drophead" is named for the coupe's special soft top.

You expect the best from a Rolls-Royce, but the Phantom Drophead is something extra special. This big coupe handles the road smoothly and has a V12 engine that can cruise from 0 to 60 mph (96.6 kph) in 5.6 seconds. Each car is hand-built to order, and the soft leather seats alone take two weeks to hand stitch. That's pure quality. Never mind "Drophead"—this coupe is drop-*dead* gorgeous!

COOL FACTS

- Car: Phantom Drophead Coupe
- Top speed: 149 mph (240 kph)
- 0–60 mph (96.6 kph): 5.6 seconds
- Power: 453 bhp
- Engine: 6.75-liter V12
- Transmission: 6-speed
- Cost: $480,000

Under the hood is a V12 engine. Traveling at 70 mph (112 kph) uses less than 10 percent of the car's power.

The Rolls-Royce "Flying Lady" is one of the most famous of all car emblems. And even better, it retracts to prevent it from being stolen.

The car door is hinged at the back. This means it can open to let passengers use both the front and back seats.

The Drophead Coupe comes in 16 regular paint colors. Or you can have them mix a special color just for you.

The Phantom Drophead is a luxury car. It is also close to the ground, making it surprisingly sporty.

The Phantom Coupe weighs more than 2½ tons, but it can handle any road conditions.

Ferrari F430

This world-famous car company was founded by race-car enthusiast Enzo Ferrari in 1929. Within 20 years, he was building sports cars for the road. Made for speed, the Ferrari F430 is everything a sports car should be. It is lightning-quick and thrilling to drive—like a real race car.

This car goes fast enough ▶ to take off! But its shape channels the air, which pushes the car down.

The F430 gets its name from its impressive sporty 4.3-liter engine.

COOL FACTS

- Car: F430
- Top speed: 196 mph (315 kph)
- 0–60 mph (96.6 kph): 4.0 seconds
- Power: 490 bhp
- Engine: 4.3-liter V8
- Transmission: 6-speed
- Cost: $200,000

Usually seen in the classic red, the F430 also comes in a sleek yellow version.

Show it off! You can see the powerful red **V8** engine through the back window.

Aston Martin DBS

British car-maker Aston Martin is well-known for building stunning sports cars. Think of the supercool 1960s Aston Martin DB5, the famous James Bond car. It was smooth and sleek, and made heads turn. Now, Aston Martin has another superstar car, the 6-liter DBS V12. This beauty can match the original for style and looks.

The hand-built V12 engine is placed in front of the driver.

◁ *The Aston Martin car company has been making cool cars since 1913.*

COOL FACTS

- Car: DBS
- Top speed: 190 mph (305 kph)
- 0–60 mph (100 kph): 4.3 seconds
- Power: 510 bhp
- Engine: 6-liter V12
- Transmission: 6-speed
- **Cost: $285,000**

Just look at the flowing lines of this beautiful, aerodynamic car. It is difficult to find a sleeker-looking body.

With a soft, black leather base, the short, chunky gear stick helps you glide through the six gears with ease.

The car body is made of a mixture of aluminum and carbon fiber. It is tough, but very light.

29

Cool Cars, Cool Features

Use your imagination. What would be the coolest special feature that a car could have? How about a type of "skin" that was **flexible** enough to move so the car could actually change shape? Or a car you could use as a boat when you wanted to? Perhaps you just want to sit in the **cockpit** of a car that can go faster than the speed of sound? Check out the cool features of these cars.

▽ This BMW concept car is dressed to impress. It is covered in a clingy material.

Unlike everyday cars that have many panels, including the doors and quarter panels, this car has just four panels: hood, trunk, and two sides.

Motors pull the fabric back to reveal the headlamps.

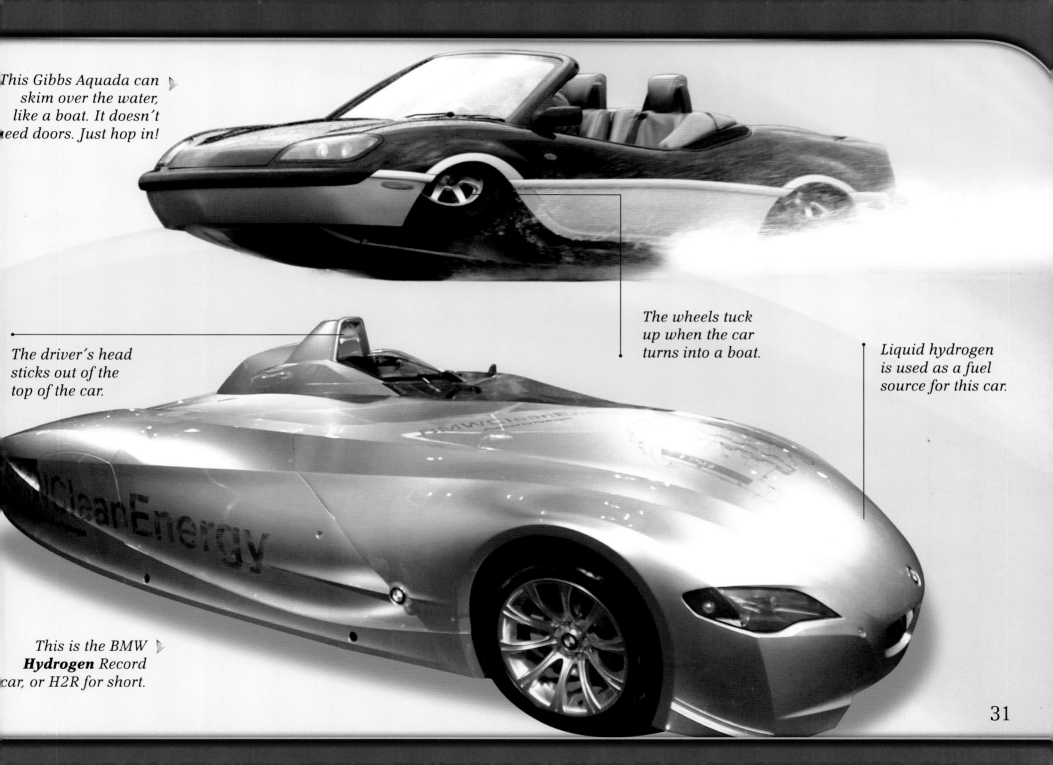

This Gibbs Aquada can skim over the water, like a boat. It doesn't need doors. Just hop in!

The wheels tuck up when the car turns into a boat.

Liquid hydrogen is used as a fuel source for this car.

The driver's head sticks out of the top of the car.

This is the BMW **Hydrogen** *Record car, or H2R for short.*

31

BMW GINA

The BMW GINA was built to explore new ideas for the road. Rather than the metal or carbon-fiber exterior that regular automobiles have, BMW's special **concept car** has a strange, stretchy, silver "skin." At the flick of a switch, the GINA's wire frame moves to change the car's body shape. Wow! It is not an alien-style car as such, but this car can certainly shape-shift.

That's original! The "skin" peels back to reveal the car's engine.

The slits covering the headlamps can either open or close. The driver controls them from inside the car.

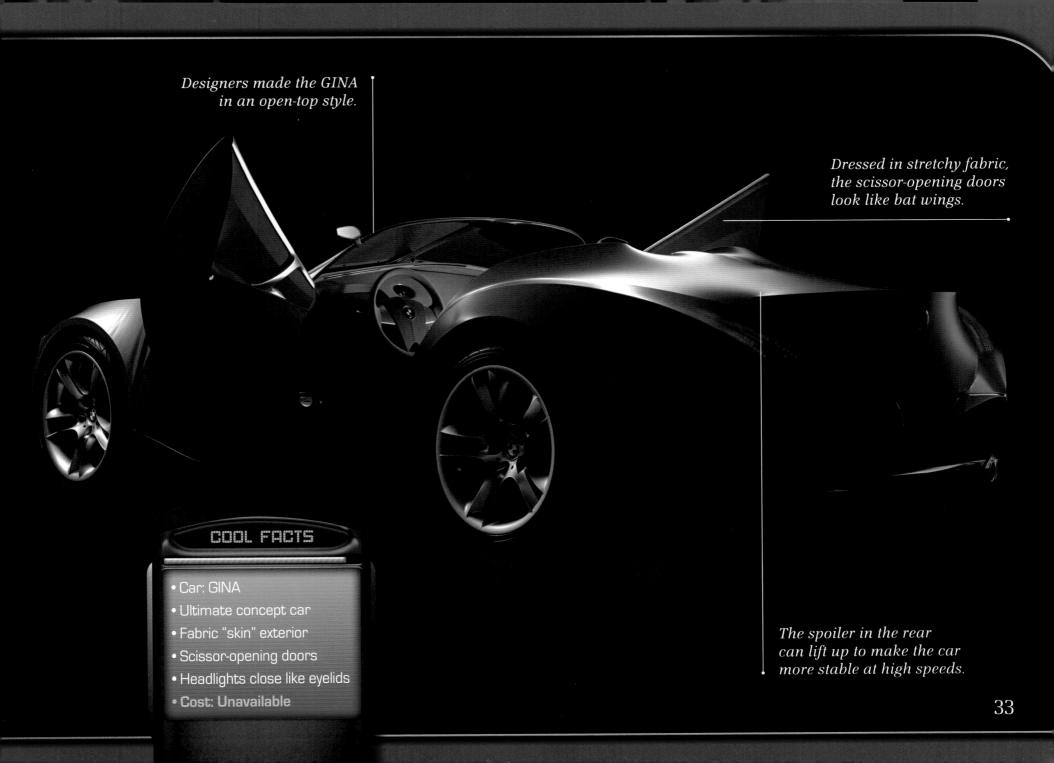

Designers made the GINA in an open-top style.

Dressed in stretchy fabric, the scissor-opening doors look like bat wings.

The spoiler in the rear can lift up to make the car more stable at high speeds.

COOL FACTS

- Car: GINA
- Ultimate concept car
- Fabric "skin" exterior
- Scissor-opening doors
- Headlights close like eyelids
- **Cost: Unavailable**

Gibbs Aquada

The Gibbs Aquada is like no other supercar in the world. This sporty little machine can travel at speeds of about 100 mph (161 kph) on roads. And if you head for the coast for some surfing, you can drive this cool vehicle straight into the ocean!

▽ *This High Speed **Amphibian** (HSA) craft sounds serious. The fun part is the car actually floats on water.*

Hook up to tow a water-skier behind the car.

The driver sits in the ▷ center of the front seat.

COOL FACTS

- Car: Aquada
- Top speed (land): 100 mph (161 kph)+
- Top speed (water): 30 mph (48 kph)+
- Power: 175 bhp
- Engine: 2.5-liter V6
- Transmission: 5-speed auto
- Cost: $240,000

To drive the car back onto land, the driver throws a switch to drop the wheels down.

BMW H2R

This sleek, shiny, space-age craft is a **dual-fuel car**, so it is **environment friendly**. Able to run on hydrogen or gasoline for extra power, the aerodynamic BMW H2R was built for racing. Although it looks like it has just rolled off the factory floor, this silver bullet was made in 2006. It quickly set many records for hydrogen cars, including the **flying-start** mile in under 20 seconds.

The aerodynamic body means air flows over the car easily.

Although the car has only three wheels, it is extremely stable at high speeds.

A record-breaker, the H2R car was built in record time, too—just 10 months.

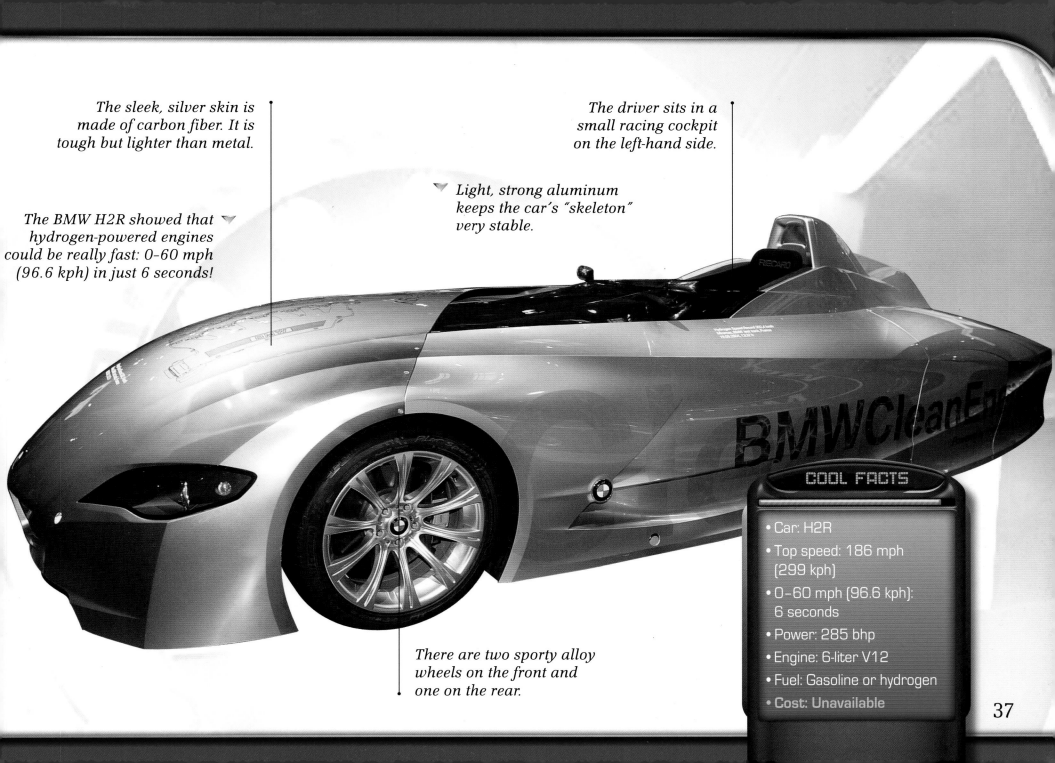

The sleek, silver skin is made of carbon fiber. It is tough but lighter than metal.

The BMW H2R showed that hydrogen-powered engines could be really fast: 0–60 mph (96.6 kph) in just 6 seconds!

The driver sits in a small racing cockpit on the left-hand side.

Light, strong aluminum keeps the car's "skeleton" very stable.

There are two sporty alloy wheels on the front and one on the rear.

COOL FACTS

- Car: H2R
- Top speed: 186 mph (299 kph)
- 0–60 mph (96.6 kph): 6 seconds
- Power: 285 bhp
- Engine: 6-liter V12
- Fuel: Gasoline or hydrogen
- Cost: Unavailable

Rinspeed sQuba

How cool is a car that glides through the water like a submarine? It may seem like science fiction, but this car does exist! The Rinspeed sQuba is the world's first car that can be driven both on land and underwater. Remember to wear your diving suit!

Drive the car into the water and it floats. Open the door to let the water in and start "diving" underwater.

The Rinspeed sQuba has three motors in the rear: one for land and two for water.

COOL FACTS

- Car: sQuba
- Top speed (land): 75 mph (121 kph)
- Top speed (underwater): 2 mph (3 kph)
- Engine: Electric, using rechargeable batteries
- Transmission: Rear-wheel drive (on land); two water jets, two propellers (under water)
- Power: 72 bhp
- Chassis: Based on Lotus Elise
- Cost: **$1.5 million**

The open-top design is ideal for sunny days. It is also necessary for safety underwater—and a car with a roof would float for a short time.

There is a powerful jet drive on each side.

The all-electric Rinspeed sQuba produces no exhaust emissions at all.

The car's lights are powerful, yet energy-efficient, **LED**s.

Thrust SSC

Is that really a car? It looks more like a rocket or an airplane, but the Thrust SSC is a car—SSC stands for SuperSonic Car, and this car has traveled at 763 mph (1,228 kph). That's supersonic, or faster than the speed of sound, which is as fast as some jet airplanes!

▽ *On its record-breaking run, the Thrust SSC was traveling faster than the noise it was making!*

The cockpit is centrally located between the two massive engines.

▽ *The Thrust SSC needed a parachute attached to the rear to slow it down.*

The Thrust SSC is powered by two enormous jet engines.

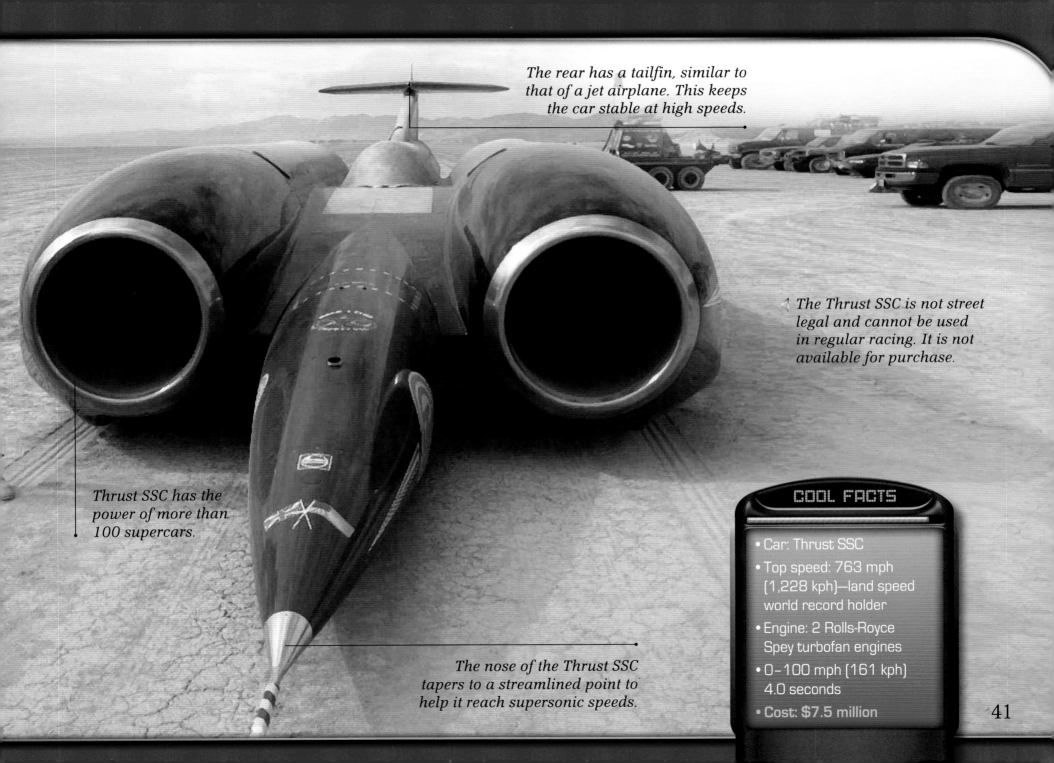

The rear has a tailfin, similar to that of a jet airplane. This keeps the car stable at high speeds.

The Thrust SSC is not street legal and cannot be used in regular racing. It is not available for purchase.

Thrust SSC has the power of more than 100 supercars.

The nose of the Thrust SSC tapers to a streamlined point to help it reach supersonic speeds.

COOL FACTS

- Car: Thrust SSC
- Top speed: 763 mph (1,228 kph)—land speed world record holder
- Engine: 2 Rolls-Royce Spey turbofan engines
- 0–100 mph (161 kph) 4.0 seconds
- Cost: $7.5 million

Supercars for Superstars

Many celebrities and sports superstars own dream cars like the ones in this book. Some of them own several.

Singer Beyoncé uses a Rolls-Royce convertible to arrive at a concert in classic style.

Superstar	Job	Supercar
Akon	Musician	Lamborghini Murciélago Roadster
Criss Angel	Magician Superstar	Bugatti Veyron, Rolls-Royce, Porsche Turbo
David Beckham	Soccer	Porsche Turbo
Kobe Bryant	Basketball—LA Lakers	Ferrari 458 Italia Lamborghini Aventador
Simon Cowell	TV Personality/Producer	Bugatti Veyron Super Sport
Flo-Rida	Singer/Songwriter	Bugatti Veyron Ferrari California
Ice-T	Actor/Musician	Aston Martin Vantage
Rampage Jackson	MMA/UFC fighter	Lamborghini LP640 Spyder
Lebron James	Basketball	Ferrari F430 & Camaro SS
Jay-Z	Musician	Bugatti Veyron Grand Sport
Michael Jordan	Basketball—retired	Mercedes-Benz SLR 722
Beyoncé Knowles	Musician/Actor	Mercedes-Benz S-Class
Ashton Kutcher	Actor	Fisker Karma
Bucky Lasek	Extreme Sports—skateboard	996 Porsche Turbo
Rafael Nadal	Tennis	Aston Martin DBS
Ozzy Osbourne	Musician	Ferrari 458 Italia
Michael Phelps	Olympic Swimmer	BMW 7 Series
Clinton Portis	Football	Maserati Gran Turismo
Cristiano Ronaldo	Soccer	Lamborghini Aventador LP700-4
Ryan Seacrest	TV & Radio Personality/Producer	Aston Martin DB9
Michael Strahan	Football—retired	Aston Martin V12 Vanquish
Sasha Vujacic	Basketball	Mercedes-Benz SL550 & Lamborghini LP640
Mark Wahlberg	Actor	Lamborghini Diablo SE30
Kanye West	Musician	Mercedes-Benz S-Class
Shaun White	Olympic Snowboarder	Lamborghini LP640
Mark Zuckerberg	CEO, Facebook	Acura TSX

▲ David Beckham loves great cars. Here he is driving a Porsche, with his wife Victoria.

▲ This chrome-painted Fisker Karma belongs to Justin Bieber.

Supercar Superfacts

Check out some of these amazing facts about the world's most awesome cars!

Most expensive supercars

Bugatti Veyron Super Sport	$2.4 million
Pagani Zonda Cinque Roadster	$1.85 million
Aston Martin One-77	$1.85 million
Lamborghini Reventón	$1.6 million
Koenigsegg Agera R	$1.6 million
Maybach Landaulet	$1.38 million
Zenvo ST1	$1.225 million
McLaren F1	$970,000
Ferrari Enzo	$670,000
Pagani Zonda C12 F	$667,000

World's most expensive car

In 2012, a 1962 Ferrari GTO 250 sold for $35 million, making it the planet's most expensive car.

Gold star car

Supercar McLaren F1's engine has a gold-plated lining. The gold is not just for showing off—it reflects the heat of the engine better than other metals.

Super drivers

In 1963, Craig Breedlove reached the speed of 408 mph (657 kph) in Spirit of America. The U.S. drivers held the land speed record for 20 years until British driver Richard Noble drove Thrust 2 to a speed of 633 mph (1,019 kph). The record was smashed by Thrust SSC (another Richard Noble car) in 1997. This time the car was driven by fighter pilot Andy Green.

Vanity plates

Vanity plates or customized license plates are plates that have letters and numbers chosen by the owners. Usually the letters and numbers are carefully arranged so they look like the owner's name or are the owner's initials and birth date. Vanity plates can cost thousands of dollars. The world's most expensive vanity plate is "1." It was sold in Abu Dhabi for $14.5 million in 2008.

Supercar Superwords

aerodynamic
having a smooth shape, so that air can pass over easily

amphibian
a type of animal, or vehicle, that can cope with both land and water

bhp
short for "brake horse power"; it is the energy that the engine creates on its own

carbon fiber
a very strong, light material often used to build the car body

chassis
the frame that supports the body of a car

chauffeur
a person who drives someone around

cockpit
a space in the car for the driver

concept car
an "idea" car, often built for car shows

convertible
a car with a roof that can come off

coupe
usually a hard-top sports car

cylinder
one of many tube-shaped parts inside a car engine, where fuel is burned

dual-fuel car
a car that can work using two different types of fuel

environmentally friendly
something that doesn't harm the natural world

flexible
bendable

flying start
a racing start in which the car is already moving when it crosses the starting line

hard-top
a type of car with a hard roof

hatchbacks
cars with an extra door at the rear

hydrogen
a type of fuel used to power some cars

hypercar
a car that is even more expensive than a supercar

kph
short for kilometers per hour; this is a metric measurement to show how fast a car can travel

LED
a device that produces a light on electrical and electronic equipment

limited edition
a special type of car, when only a few are made

low-profile tires
sporty, modern tires that are low and wide

manufacturer
a person or business that makes a product

mph
short for miles per hour; this measurement shows you just how fast a vehicle is moving

production car
a car usually built in large numbers for general sale

sedan

a car with four or six seats

sports car

a small car that is extremely quick
and fun to drive

stealth fighter jet

a special type of jet plane that is designed
so that it can fly through radar almost as
if it is invisible

supercar

a very expensive, powerful sports car

transmission

the gears and parts that connect
a car's engine to its wheels

twin-turbo engine

an engine using not one, but two
turbochargers to create even more power

V8

a type of car engine, with 8 cylinders
arranged like a letter V

V12

a type of car engine, with 12 cylinders
arranged like a letter V

W16

a mega supercar engine with cylinders
arranged like a W—that is like having
two V8 engines stuck together

Index